Umbrellas or Else

Umbrellas or Else

Poems

J DIEGO FREY

AN IMPRINT OF BOWER HOUSE

DENVER

Cover Design by Sonya Unrein

Library of Congress Cataloging-in-Publication Data
is available upon request.

ISBN: 978-1-938633-47-8

10 9 8 7 6 5 4 3 2

Grateful acknowledgment is made to Sarah, without whom the author probably would still be selling himself and his poetry far too short. Also thanks to the Moose and the Squid, who sometimes don't climb on the author when he's writing.

The author owes a great debt to the hard-working members of the Battery Group and of Poets Beyond Reason who put up with my nonsense for far too long. Also thanks to Lighthouse Writers Workshop and the excellent guidance of Chris, Micheal and Andrea.

Some of the poems in this collection have appeared in print before in various magazines and online journals, including:

- WAZEEJOURNAL.ORG ("Where I Go at Night" and "The Saint of Enclosed Spaces")

- SALON.COM ("Narcissus Trims His Nosehair")

- *Thirteen Hills* ("Wilbik")

- *Sarasota Review of Poetry* ("In Eternity Out with Kelly")

- *Mobius: The Journal of Social Change* ("Back Page of the Free Weekly Newspaper, Englewood, Colorado, December 7, 1996")

for Henrys

"My great-grandfather . . . is attributed [with] the inexplicable imprecation, 'C'ai takeissa 'na medà meshônà faita a paraqua.' ('May he have an accident shaped like an umbrella')."

—Primo Levi, "The Periodic Table"

"Our camel, he said, had a bad case of gleeks
And should lie flat in bed for at least twenty weeks."

—Dr. Seuss, "I Had Trouble in Getting to Solla Sollew"

TABLE OF CONTENTS

part one

brief intermission

part two

part one

"I am nutpaste . . ."

The Persistence of the Oxygen Tank Man Waiting to Cross Fillmore Avenue at the Last Stoplight before Your House

You kids quitcher goddam babooning!

Yer shouting, gespouting
yer rasping and mooning.

Not so goddam
special,
yer not.

With yer gold-ducked satchels
and yer pet pachyderms
yer snowjob grouting
and yer popsicle sperms.

You don't know the cold from the kelvin . . .

When I was yer age,
we all lived on Mars.
And everyone had the same enemy.
We named every boy the same name: Melvin.
And all the girls were called
Anemone.

And it was so cold the silk
would stick to the worms.

We didn't have yer
volcano sportscars
and yer lemon
verbena nachos.

You kids don't know the meaning of the meaning of
    the meaning of . . .

Hear this:
someday, words my marks,
all these pouting lights're going out.
And then, oh yes, by God,
then you bastards out here gleaning love
are gonna learn
what the barking's all about.

Dammed if I wouldn't tell you m'self.

And I would
if I didn't . . . nope.
Didn't have this thing,
this else,
this pope,
pressing down on me
here
right above
my left cantaloupe.

Tenderfoot

Civilization,
or just civil conversation,
ended
after you left me
there at that diner
to finish the rest of the onion rings.

I was, we were
on the western edge of Nebraska
somehow part of a Veterans' Day parade
celebrating wars
I'd never studied in high school.

And maybe it's how you shrieked
in frustration
or just the irresistible look
of someone else's girlfriend
storming off in anger,
but the officers and enlisted men
took notice,
took an instant dislike to me.

Now curious and menacing
this pack of ex-soldiers
with no legs
they pursue me
through deserted, post-facto, prairie townscapes,

past the shattered fives-and-dime
where oxen-eyed shopgirls peer from behind
empty glass counters,
past weedy town squares,
and post offices long since painted black.

Legless, bald
with shiny red faces, the color of wax around cheese
they had tied kerchiefs
to their necks like gunslingers.

My mama always predicted this.

"Pump your gasoline and get out,"
she'd warn.
"No good comes to folks who linger
in filling stations."

That
is what I think of:
my mom,
and your parting sneer

on the run
from these bellowing wheelchairs.

Visitor

I have not come to consume—
the open trawler of my credit cards
scooping up all my covets.

I have not come to crown myself king,
to assume my rightful place
on the unburnished throne
of the new century.

I have not come on a mission.
Not looking to convert the pagans,
divert the enemy,
subvert the dominant paradigm.

I didn't show up here to sing,
chirp, complain, ply anything
resembling troth.

This isn't a social call
so we can all stop smiling.

I do not wish to learn
any valuable lessons
or listen to anyone's goddamn
life story.

I will not be making a scene,
amends,
change for a twenty,
or advances on anyone's wife.

I will not be bringing
the audience to its feet.

Just point me
towards the closest room
containing functional indoor plumbing
and I'll be on my way.

Yes, a sink will suffice.

Diner of Too Much Significance

The Elephant of Impatience
hunches over a booth
in the Coffee Shop of What's Your Hurry.

Without meaning to,
he has parked himself again at the station
of the Waitress of Destiny's Sarcasm.

Two Old Ladies of Get Out Much?
are struggling with their order
from the one-page breakfast menu.

He drums his nubbly fingers
on the Formica from an Unlamented Past,
glares in their direction.

Waitress walks up, wipes down the table,
pours him a cup of the Coffee of Much Earlier That Morning
(black, two sugars).

He orders: the Eggs that Run with Sadness,
toast and the Hash Browns.
The coffee is burning his esophagus.

All the Bad Decisions and the Sorry I Squashed Thats,
all the Don't Look in Theres
and the Yes Mother I'll Clean It Right Ups . . .

Has it all been worth it?
The Tiny Beep of Unfathomable Casios
flicks him by the left ear back to Now.

He stands up,
flings a Five-Dollar Bill of Discontent
on the table, stamps out.

There is a Bus to Catch and a job,
a Boss Who Facilitates
with Menial Tasks and Demeaning Praise.

The waitress wipes down the table.
He will be back tomorrow, same time,
at the Lunch Rush of Infinite Recurrence.

All Fall

December I think was especially hard:
we lost twenty moms and some cattle.

November dealt us a cruel deck of cards.
Nearly cost half the war in one battle.

October devised itself seasonably cold,
the restaurants cross-hatched with ice.

September your jokes got especially old
and the audience laughed only twice.

In August our wagons got stuck in some sand
when Ted sent us out for the milk.

July spoke of lies to the heart and the hand
betrayal by men made of silk.

The rest of the year I can scarcely recount,
though you bring it up each time I see you . . .

Suffice it to say that we spent your amount
on a lifestyle attempting to be you.

Truth is the Club that Knocks Down
  ## and Kills Everybody

If only someone
anyone
had spoken up about the donut crumb earlier.

Surely she deserved that much consideration.
First day on the job
taking over for the previous boss
who left amid scandal
and a psychotic breakdown.

Trying to make a good impression
box of glazed and chocolate
at the staff meeting
where it all went wrong.

And she was all right
bantering easily about the high points of last quarter
telling a humorous story
about the elevators
when a chunk of pastry
an outrider from the oversized cruller
she was chewing
leapt sideways to escape her mouth
and landed
two-thirds of the way up her left cheek.

It just sat there, like it was home from work.

A tiny brown meal
the shape of the state of West Virginia
it bobbed up and down
to the rhythm of her conversation.

The new merit raise policy
the fundraising efforts already underway
smiling talking
the donut republic rising and falling.

We became withdrawn.

Answering her questions with monosyllables
unable to meet her gaze
to a one
our eyes locked on the wog.

Its terrible terrible tenacity
and our silent collective scream
"JUMP!"

By the time the meeting was over
and the surveys were being passed around
the catatonic staff
stumbled out of the room
fled for their cubicles and corners
to gather themselves.

Nobody had said a word.
Nobody had attempted the subconscious
I brush my face in a vigorous ear-to-nose motion
you brush yours maneuver.

She scooped up her files and headed for the ladies' room.

To this day, none of us are certain
if the donut crumb hung on
the whole way down the hall
and through the solid swinging wooden door.
A futile search party scoured the carpet
after work but before the vacuum cleaners came by.

Just that . . .

the firings began almost first thing the next day.

Life Goal #31

When I finally jello-wrestle
Barbara Walters,

I'll hit her hard.
I will not falter.

I'll pile-drive and somersault her.

I'll eat the lunch
of Barbara Walters.

2 Triolets

Double Plet

The pitcher gloves it, flips to first
and first base throws to second.
Coach in dugout fears the worst.
The pitcher gloves it, flips to first.
The batter swung a sudden burst.
Distant left field wall had beckoned.
The pitcher gloves it, flips to first
and first base throws to second.

Combat Pet

Unless it's for a slingshot fight
I'll take one thin dime over two fat nickels.
It's worth as much, four times as light.
So except for in a slingshot fight
(though I know to fight is not polite)
the dime's more economical.
Unless it's for a slingshot fight
it's one thin dime for me, not nickels.

Back Page of the Free Weekly Newspaper, Englewood, Colorado, May 8, 2005

Zippy the Pinhead leers at Zerbeena
(yellow-and-orange spotted muumuu—Fab!)
Xenon for your clear glass grow lamps. FAC
with live music from Dennis and
Vera, "Denver's Best Covers of Capt. and Tennille!"
"'Uncle' seeks friendly 'Aunt'" — the subject of
this week's featured personal ad. Drag/
Stag/or PFLAG night at "The Church."
Rental property: cat-friendly, Hawaii,
quiet street, fresh eggs and OJ
placed by your door, nearby dock.
Old tennis shoes and mousepads? Landfill
no more! (We recycle 'em!)
Mixed-breed puppies, blue and brown,
long-tailed, short legs. Pro
kayaking lessons. "It's time to stop
joking around! U.S. out of Iraq!"
Itching, chafing? Stop wearing underwear!
Hyperventilate your way to stock market riches.
Gecko feed—$8.99/pound. Thought
forming above Zippy's muumuu:
"Extra maple syrup—Zow!" (POV
directed through the glass counter from below,
creates the illusion of sex,
bacon, pancakes, and pinheadese simultaneously
above the donuts. Ad for live jazz.

Fingers and Bones

Fingers and Bones,
far from their homes,
milling through crowds
in Times Square.

Fingers remembers to
check for his messages
and Bones runs her hands
through her hair.

Over the coats of
the sailors on leave,
Fingers blows bubbles of soap.

Under a cap of
remarkable weave,
Bones spies an off-duty Pope.

She whistles to Fingers,
a snake charming sound,
that the Pontiff
is part of the revels.

But the crowd closes up
where her vision was found,
and she's pointing
her fingers at devils.

Post-Ranitadine

"When will all this white noise cease, or
change colors at least?"

The settling contents of our
shipping container
made it seem like not enough
had been sent in the first place.

Baseballs, volleyballs, or tether
they all plagued our childhood
with their demands to be flogged.

It must have been a blind ferryman
who took us, newly dead
across the river of India ink,
because he left his dog on the bank,
baying sadly out of three mouths.

Never with alcohol, unless
prescribed by a doctor.
Get me another doctor.

The sun is setting over Palestine,
Texas, and nobody notices.
Air pollution
gives us such beautiful sunsets.

Man pretended he could fly.
And God pretended not to mind.
The laws of physics, thermodynamics
and gravity proved us all to be
rather shortsighted.

I'll take my martini with just
the smallest refraction of vermouth.

Ashbery, where did you leave your wallet?

Ungulate Show

For some kids I know

Tonight I stand before you with this fleeting sense of drama
to announce a sort of disappointing fact:
our honored guest tonight will be a llama,

instead of, as was advertised, Senator Obama.
A misprint in the fine print, page six of his contract,
scuttled his appearance with eleventh-hour drama.

It seems we'd said the show would be taped in Yokahama.
Not true, we tape in Yonkers, but by then our knicks were knacked.
Thus our guest slot opened up. We called the llama.

Of course we'd meant to call (instead) the Dalai Lama
but their numbers in the phone book, back-to-back.
A big break for the llama despite the drama.

Good story, though, and he's really quite a charmer.
So tonight we go ahead with plans to reenact
scenes from the movie "Gandhi." (Mahatma played by llama.)

Thanks again to our sponsors: Al Paca's Wool-O-Rama,
upon whose strong suggestion our legal team was sacked.
And now let's start the show with no more drama:
our honored guest tonight will be a llama.

19

Men Have Such Interesting Problems

For my wife's therapist

This one buys shoes just to get his feet rubbed.

This one has a fetish for armpits.

This one's not happy until he is scrubbed
by a dominant woman named Brigit.

This one was beaten when he was a boy.

This one was dressed as a sailor.

This one still plays with his G.I. Joe toys.

This one's in love with his tailor.

This one reminisces his first wife too much,
how she dumped him to date Norman Mailer.

This one can't choose between Starsky and Hutch,
Oscar and Felix, Stimpy and Ren.

This one would like it if you'd let him watch.

This one is President of the Senate Protemp.

This one at six saw his parents have sex.

This one is plain scared of love.

This one's a mystery writer named Rex.

This one refers to his penis as Jub-Jub
and takes Zoloft just for the side effects.

A Steady Diet of Cheap Viagra

Tangled, woven, deceitful, this our modern web
with its terrific and terrible effluence.
Each day delivers new messages, somehow sent to nobody—
bearing Byzantine requests from barristers in need,
or instant social help for men with too short legs.
And all too often, alarmingly, they are emailed by my mother.

This is not to say that I am not fond of my mother
or that I blame her in any way for this false web
of promises arriving on electric legs.
Nero had aqueducts to remove the effluence
of human waste. Two millennia later, we seem to need
to retain it in folders marked "nobody."

Thus, despite my sincere wish to correspond with nobody
I am afforded, through the offices of my mother,
access to the thoughts of the millions who need
to share the day's catch from their cortical webs.
I am offered penis growth and ready affluence,
promised free porn of the breasts, ears, pancreas, legs.

Sure, occasionally a useful leggy
list of trivia—the sort of items that nobody
you know knows: how to catch a squirrel in your flue and
what was invented by Monica Lewinsky's mother.
What happened to the images of the marble bust that wept?
What gangsta rap song gives props to old Sam Snead?

How handy to have explained why a cat kneads
its bed! Twenty-six bones make up the human leg.
More about that LSD spider and its recursive web?
Or how about winning lottery ticket still claimed by nobody?
Mental message senders, named by demented mothers,
use psychotic subject headings that don't bother with a fluency

in English, Canadian, Portuguese. The effluence
    of spell-check sewage like "v1ag4ra" and "aw3$0me P3n1s"
    needs
sifting by the most ironic of shovels. These mothers
    who have named their children Slagpit O. Equity or
    Consuela Leg,
Felicity Tantamount or Viewpoint C. Nobody,
    have surely strayed too long in the psychedelic spider's
    web.

A brave new effluence arrives on hairy binary legs—
so much that we all earnestly need, so very little there
    for nobody.
Sometimes I miss my mother though, spinning off in her
    distant web.

Playground

Vishnu smiles,
holds up his left index finger
as if to say
we're number one, dude.
His backwards baseball
cap spins
forward occasionally
to reveal its terrible
cloth teeth.

My buddy Buddha and I
have just pulled up
to the playground
on our twin Schwinns,
eager to strike up
a friendly game of Lotus Tag
or, if Ganesh will play catcher,
kickball.

On the swings Isis
and Osiris
sing a nursery rhyme
about floods, plagues
and the annihilation of all life.

Kali is alone again,
pushing herself up on one end
of the seesaw
and then just letting herself
fall back to the ground
with a great, shattering thud
that sends grown men
screaming
across the soccer fields.

365 Years of Trivial Arguments

Catalogs of cheeseburgers and regret
Dripping fast through a clenched fist
Ten tents in a field blown down
Overweight gods on the TV set

Dripping fast through my clenched fist
What slips away are things we keep
Overweight gods squash the TV set
How we own the accomplishments we list

What slips away what we should keep
Juice the looks and tastes like blood
Our accomplishments will form a list
Five, counting sex with a sheep

Juice that looks and tastes like blood
And an expensive sweater on Satan
Five, last he counted, and sex with a sheep
What's meant by chewing one's cud

Satan in cashmere starting to sweat
Ten tents arrayed in unholy field
Chewing on something describes it just partly
Listed with cheeseburgers, lust, and regret

Unravel

For Mimi S.

Weaving to a stand
on the commuter train,
a bulbous roseate man
informs us from his sad mustache
that his soul is in flames.

We are far more concerned,
however,
about the ominous, half-fastened
state of his trousers.

Why We Don't Go Out

We don't likes to go
into other folk's houses
'cause there's no telling
whats we could find.

There's porn-o-graphic magazines,
and often nervous, angry scenes,
and mouse leavings
where we has dined.

We don't likes to drop in
on those other's lives
when we don't understands
all their gestures.

They quakes with their lips,
and they shakes with their fists
and they tells us rude things
'bout their sisters.

We won't take a trip in a trailer with friends
who uses their means justified by their ends.

We won't settle down to a tense game of bridge
when the host keeps the hostess's head in the fridge.

There's only so much, see,
that our peoples can takes.
And it's too much to ask them
old habits to breaks.

And there's so much that
other folks brings to the table,
beyond what is sane,
beyond what is stable,
beyond what is normally accepted behavior.

So we looks to our own when we looks for our savior.

Tarantula

Not the spider,
but the idea of it,
outstretched like the fingers
of an unwelcome handshake,

scarabing down the wall
and across
to the dim circle
of light

surrounding the small green area
rug green
and red and green

in which my chair
and I cringe
at this greeting

steadily advancing
on
its
hairy thoughts.

Generic Love Poem with Leaky Dishwasher

The steady drip of days that pass
does nothing to rinse out your leaving.
Watery orange juice in a dirty glass
and the tasteless oatmeal of grieving
array themselves in this sorry tableau
against the beige of the early afternoon sun.
Over eggs my voice had cracked "Don't go!"
(The kitchen remodel was only half done...)

But that stubborn leaking of tears has been fixed
here at the end of summer.
And as the caulking and grouting and epoxy get mixed,
I've become quite attached to the plumber.
He's older than you and not as soft-skinned
but he understands just what I need.
It's also a comfort that he smiles at me often
and his work is twelve months guaranteed.

2 More Triolets

No Horseplet
You kids knock it off before someone gets hurt—
this smacking, grab-assing, and general mirth.
I've just finished sweeping and you're covered with dirt.
You kids knock it off before someone gets hurt.
You're acting like monkeys when monkeys revert.
So before I start beating you for all you are worth,
you kids knock it off before someone gets hurt—
this smacking, grab-assing, and general mirth.

Elly-Met
Hillbilly goddess moved to L.A.
when her Uncle Jed shot at some oil.
She would've said tri-o-lett, not tri-o-lay,
this hillbilly goddess moved to L.A.,
but I would've allowed her to pronounce it that way.
(As her boyfriend I could have been that kind of loyal.)
Hillbilly goddess moved to L.A.
when her Uncle Jed shot at some oil.

Rebus

Familiar, terrible moment

when we are
between activities
snacking on salted peanuts
in the shell.

End of autumn afternoon
sun warming
this quiet plaza
to a pleasant yellow hue.

And I think about the
Spanish wall,
the square ceramic tiles
pressed red and green and yellow and orange
into the stucco of the community center

as if they were a child's game
a rebus
that I could rearrange with my thumbs
sliding them around
in straight lines
until the picture
of a happy future
emerged.

"Do you ever think about our Future?"
You're looking at me through
squinting serious eyes.

Hesitation.
"The peanut is neither a nut, nor a pea," I reply,
not sure whether it was your eyes
or the question
that herded me onto that
non-sequitur.

The sinking feeling
that once again we are at that place
in the subtle
taxonomy of our relationship.

The place I've come to refer to as
"Mrs. Jones is pissed."

Broccoli Dream

In which you are standing at the sink
trying to douse a fire
of flaming broccoli

as I stand by
watching
not helping, just observing, unable not to smile.

If there's an answer, a meaning
to this dream
(and I sort of hope there isn't, though I will venture to guess
anyway)
then I don't think it means that
your head or my head is on fire.

Broccoli comes in bunches,
not heads.
That's cabbage that you're thinking of.

Nor do I think broccoli is meant
to represent wealth
as it is a common vegetable.

It isn't necessarily nature,
or the urge to a more natural existence.
Not healthy eating,
nor a rebuke of Republican presidents.

It won't stand in for any of those things,
not even for the part of me that is shaped
sort of like broccoli—
that part of me people comment on only
after they have known me,
and showered with me,
for a good, long time.

What I really prefer to choose,
if this nighttime visitation
has any meaning at all,
is this:

You are to stand for you.
I am to stand for I.
And the broccoli, well

that's supposed to stand for something
that's not supposed to
ever
catch fire.

You are fighting an impossible blaze
and I am stuck watching,

awestruck at the sight
of the gorgeous smokeless
green flames.

Bruce

Cattlecar, chicken car, people car caboose.
I like red wine.
You like red wine.
We drink beer with Bruce.

Storage building, office building, luggage rack museum.
I have no time.
You have no time.
Bruce is on per diem.

Elementary, tertiary, seventh manifold.
I'm remorseful.
You're remorseful.
Bruce keeps us on hold.

Doppelganger, pterodactyl, ectoplasm scones.
I'll distract him.
You vivisect him.
Let the desert bleach his bones.

brief intermission

(about the author)

"Frosting stuck to plastic . . ."

This Was Supposed to Be a Simple Song

Tell of a shelf
upended by rain.
And the forest of kelp
that grew up in my brain.
In the night comes your yelp
(as we circle the drain):

"Umbrellas or else—
we will sing it again!"

Two Triolets Specifically about Snack Food

Fritolet
All that's left are salted shards
remaining in my post-lunch snack.
These corny planks deep-fried in lard . . .
All that's left are salted shards.
To catch the last orange communards
I tip the crinkly chip bag back.
All that's left are salted shards
remaining in my post-lunch snack.

Milkywet
This chocolate, caramel and nougat
belongs to me—you stay away.
Though lunch is gone and tempus fugit,
this chocolate, caramel and nougat
is no more for you than Xavier Cugat.
Perhaps I'll bring some more some day.
But this chocolate, caramel and nougat
is mine—you stay the hell away!

Re: The Cupcakes

I found
perched furtively
in your top
left-hand desk drawer

I have eaten them
They were delicious
though frosting
stuck to plastic

Please forgive me
as they were in
the way of
the Paterson file

cc: wcw

Haikus to a Drinking Buddy

empty beer bottle
resting by barcalounger
more friends soon join it

the way that you belched
the theme to "The Rockford Files"
is wicked skillful

did we decide I
am designated driver
oh crap! call a cab

I don't believe that
I am a homosexual
but your hair looks good

Narcissus Trims His Nosehair

For nearly thirty-seven years
I had control of nose and ears.
Smooth skin upon the conch and lobe
and nostrils clean as Manitobe.

But time and genes bedevil me.
My good health lost to revelry.
I'm sprouting gardens in these holes
profuse enough to shelter voles!

Now naked fore the glass I stand,
electric clippers in my hand,
to prune these bushes back to stumps
and check my testicles for lumps.

Exotic growths from crotch to head—
signs, at least, that I'm not dead.

About the Author

The author does not remember writing this.

The author is not God.

The author is from a small Iowa town known for its famous cannibal.

The author wrote this book in memory of his cat, Mr. Stinky-Winky.

The author doesn't believe in the Easter Bunny or the Avon Lady.

The author wrote this book wearing a bright red muumuu.

The author likes slipping the word "muumuu" into casual conversation.

The author didn't so much invent this genre as he did rip it off in a cheap and repetitive manner.

The author has recently suffered from an allergic reaction to styrofoam peanuts.

The author went to a school that emphasized an entry-level version of ethnic diversity.

The author is emotionally invested in your reaction to this book.

The author knows where you live.

The author has a photograph of you and a well-annotated list of your regular daily activities taped to the wall above his writing desk.

The author probably shouldn't have told you that.

The author is still thinking about you, wondering what you have on right now.

The author had a dream about you just last night.

In the author's dream, you were wearing a hat shaped like an inflated bratwurst.

The author has maybe said too much.

The author thinks he looks kinda bitchin' in this monocle.

The author knows better than to eat spare-ribs right before
    dinner.
The author's gastroenterologist has reminded him of this
    very issue on several occasions, usually while probing
    the author's rectum with the world's unluckiest camera.
The author is sorry.
The author wants you to know that he forgives you too.
The author deserves non-generic mayonnaise.
The author was in Montreal at the time.
Most weekday mornings, the author can be found
    on the corner of 6th and Frost, exposing his pantoums
    to passersby.
The author remains alert in his natural habitat, listening
    for the sound of approaching predators.
The author no longer wets his bed, although someone
    else's bed is still fair game.
The author prefers to wait for a cleaner restroom.
The author's coach will turn into a pumpkin at midnight,
    as will his driver turn into an iguana, his agent into
    a scared bunny rabbit, and his most recent royalty check
    into a disembodied laughing tongue.
The author put it all on Tiny Dancer to show.
The author wrote this book while he was waiting
    for his other book to be published.
The author wants to lacerate your soul with the overgrown
    fingernails of his metaphor.
The author gnaws on tree bark and bamboo in order to ingest
    the essential minerals and fiber necessary for regular
    digestive functioning during his long cold winter sleep.
The author didn't ask for all this profane beauty.
The author remembers a spring day when he was just
    a small boy and the sound of locusts, chewing, chewing.

The author knows a guy.

The author hasn't always felt like this.

There was a time, in fact, when the author was significantly more dewy-eyed and reluctant to compromise his artistic integrity.

The author can be bought today however, for the price of a dozen of those little tequila bottles that are such a blessing to him flying in and out of the Reno airport as often as he does.

The author will take whatever the fuck is behind curtain number 3.

The author continues to maintain that he didn't write this book, his talking penis did.

The author thought long and hard.

The author feels it important to floss regularly, and visit the goddam dentist once in a while.

The author has never suffered from cradle-cap, kennel-cough, or crotchrot.

The author takes great pains.

The author takes precautions.

The author takes, takes, and takes, but where is the giving?

The author could use both a bigger Speedo and a bag of Beano.

The author remembers his mother's birthday, but forgets her face.

The author stands alone.

The author ate the cheese.

The author took the cake as well.

The author, unlike many of his contemporaries, is possessed of neither an advanced degree nor a particularly interesting biography.

The author always reads the about the author section first.

The author is thinking Mexican for lunch tomorrow.

part two

"If there's an answer,
a meaning to this dream
(and I sort of hope there isn't, though
I will venture to guess anyway) . . ."

Salamanders

Or are they only newts?
Tiny aqua eyes and pink
denizens in rubber suits.
Are they in fact only newts?
Arrayed in rings around our boots,
Busby Berkeley baby skinks.
Are we gods and they just newts?
Tiny aqua eyes and pink.

Dori kneels and spreads her hands,
strokes the water, sings.
Exotic wind and rippled sands—
Dori kneels and spreads her hands.
Newts swim up to her in bands.
Tiny pink and aqua rings.
Dori kneels and spreads her hands,
strokes the water, sings.

Oedipus Rose from His Wet Dream

For Steve Hemenway

Casting aspersions of prostrate appliance,
his decorum took a dive off the bridge.

He was blinded by love and disfigured by science,
this fool, with his heart and his brain in the sink,
    and his beer and his legs in the fridge.

Those seventeen times he related his scandal:
how the creeps dressed in pink speared his orbit.

But no less the light of the seventeenth candle
could lumen his reason nor
    hatch his redemption nor
curdle the milk of his forfeit.

A surfer shot through with his love's own tsunami,
a body of water of bodies of women.

Its riptides arrived with the voice of his mommy
and the rest came to he who could ride tectonickly
    past the eyes and mouths
and the clutching fast shouts
of the drowned-and-the-dried-in-the-sea men

How to File Your Reimbursement Claim

Do not wait
as some have
for the chill of winter to arrive
paralyzing the bones of the land.
In fact, you really should
get it in the mail
sometime
in the next 30 – 60 days.

Please be aware
that the lack of a signature
will cause us
to doubt your very existence.

In the section marked
REASON FOR CLAIM
do not blacken
more than one of the six white circles.
There can only be one
reason.

And do not write in
your own reason.
Only God can make up reasons.

Alice and James See the Comet

In the year after the reign of the good Rex Felicis
a comet danced from constellation to constellation
in the sky above his grave.

I watched from a seat in the Royal Garden,
the Royal Consort on my lap,
and we remembered our fallen hero and
the way that he danced
from room to room and day to day.

The tendency in this culture is to make
a big thing about omens such as this one, but
I think it was just a small thing.
A private thing.

Between every creature who witnessed the shimmering
fire in the sky and their own memories.

Thus we sat up late last night
gazing upward,
eyes warm with tears in the chilly Spring air,
glad for the shared comfort
of each other
the past
and the small but important glisten in the night above our heads.

What Woke Us

Eventually, it was the squirrel,
his chitter cracking our repose.
Indignant with this waking world,
demanding justice for his woes.

Snarling spitter, mad mad mad,
his branch perch cold and too damn early.
Laments for love he'd never had,
for parents who were too damn squirrelly,

and outrage at our sleeping forms
at rest behind the glassy wall.
The thunder of these squirrelish storms
became our final wake-up call.

Previous the phone had
chirped,
a brief repentant sound.

Previous the cat had
burped
and leapt from bed to ground.

Previous we dreamt and swayed, our debts and dramas unrepaid,
    and lies
from birth and death extracted . . . we swam in rivers deep
    protracted, dove down into eyes and ears with epic lust
    and soaring fears, eager for that long
last drink of who we've lost and what they think.

And previous became today
the blinding chitter road.
A tree-bound rodent's hell to pay,
for sins some other squirrel had sowed.

One Possible Redeemer

Franklin's wearing his briefs again
and
tonight the whole world is at rest.
For twenty-four hours the killing will stop
while Franklin is comfortably dressed.

Franklin is wearing his briefs
again.
International economies rejoice.
After a spell of uncomfortable slippage
Frank's back in cotton by choice.

Franklin's wearing his briefs
again.
The heads of religion will cheer.
The holy crusades that marked the last era
are packed away just like Frank's gear.

O,
look to the sky
you can see Franklin spin
on civilization's high tower.
His briefs flash out whitely,
he's covered politely,
and he's recently taken a shower.

Franklin's out in his briefs again
and
the severe laws of physics can grin.
We have huddled forlorn in the closet of entropy
until Frank and his undies came in.

Finster Alley

Whatever the Tribune said,
I did not attack those nuns.

We were just in an awkward situation—that's all.

My weak bladder condition
is the first thing, in fact, that you
must've learned about me,
considering where you met me
(Finster Alley)
and what I was peeing on
(the dumpster behind your bookstore).

(You may remember that you did not
call the police.)

It was spring, I recall,
and you were wearing yellow.
The soft air strolled in from the coast,
and I saw your salmon-colored hair
enhaloed by the afternoon light.
I think I knew I loved you an instant
after I zipped my fly.

So yesterday,
when I heard the sirens ricocheting
off the stone walls of St. Catherine's,
I was naturally a bit upset.
(I said some words.
I may have gestured in a threatening manner.)

But I did not strike, or attempt to strangle, anyone.
I even offered to borrow the hose and wash off their dumpster.

Return to the Chesterfield

It was a small town,
just south of Kankakee.
Someone flushed the toilet
and all the lights went out.
The children burned the strip mall down
while Whitman wrung his yankee hanky.

Ask her to wear a big blond wig
and call her Mrs. Roosevelt.
Light up two French director's cigs
before you hit your boss below the belt.

Years later, Cat Stevens returned to America.
"The biscotti tasted like shit."

We were there in the bar
then Bruno kicked us out,
and that was all there was to it.

When the tour bus pulled in
to Pope John Paul II's
hometown of Krakow,
they all got out except
deaf old Mrs. Shulkin
who frowned:
"I do not want to see a crackhouse."

Piranhas in the Stream of Consciousness, March 2004

There is a severed head taped to the t-shirt display and a certain bitterness
to my second cup of coffee
as I realize I have spent the last
oblivious fifteen minutes
ogling the prominent breasts of the barman's girlfriend.

They are burying the Muslim dead in Iraq with their heads pointing
    toward Mecca;
mine will have to point towards the men's room, I guess.

Somebody quoted to me once
a study
that concluded the most violent place on earth
is right
behind the left forelobe
of the human brain, where
reality and fantasy
careen into each other
with the murderous intensity of bullets and bad ideas.

In Eternity Out with Kelly

She has insane, but trustworthy eyes,
like the eyes of a discredited cult leader.
They fill with blue light as she smiles,
invite me to lose myself.

When I am out with them,
she, her husband, and her eyes,
I can't meet her gaze for fear I won't return home.

". . . prevent a violent crime?" her husband asks me,
and I nod,
blankly, mired in metaphysical foreplay.

"Uh-huh. I guess so."

He smiles, satisfied.
I feel caught.

Does she know how I feel? She is all knowing,
this middle class avatar,
this brown haired married goddess.
She must know, but she denies my searching look
seats herself at the other end of the table.

Someone's mother
sitting with half a bottle of white wine
on a night that permanently changed . . .

"Speaking of stab wounds . . ." he turns back to me.

"Were we?"

She laughs.
Cruel music and
I drop quickly out of my dream
of the scent of power between her small breasts
the majestic incline of her naked shoulders
and down, down into my mortal body
which is just now reaching across the table

for my beer glass in the most casual
and natural gesture I can spontaneously create.

The Arachnophobe's Snack

I never set out to eat the spider,
more a symptom she was than the cause.
Not that I'm adverse to adventurous meals,
but scallops maybe, sushi if I'm drunk.
Certainly nothing with quite so many legs
nor quite so hairy and alive.

What does it mean to be alive?
As much for me, I guess, as for the spider.
To chase about the world on 2 to 8 legs,
to be part of the ecology, we cause
events and respond to them, sometimes drunk.
At least we always show up for meals.

But when is something you eat not a meal?
Not so much whether it is dead or alive,
as with hydroponic lettuce or blood drunk
straight from the fruit-fly's body, a la spider.
At best, a meal should be more effect than cause
just as a table is more top than legs.

Nonetheless, I should have felt the legs
walking across my cheek so unlike a meal.
And usually the panic that it would cause—
in my room (much less on my face) a live,
eight-legged, black and brown, hairy spider—
would have waked the dead. But not the dead drunk.

Admittedly, I'd lost count of how many beers I'd drunk.
Not much was clear as I wobbled to bed on rubbery legs.
This is, no doubt, why I didn't notice the spider
skulking on the ceiling, hunting for meals.
It's possible that I didn't look alive
from way up there—that may be the cause

of the arachnid's indiscretion—because
she crawled or lowered herself to my drunk,
corpse-like form. The biggest mistake of her life.

As she crossed the beach of cheek on careful legs
my sharp, inward snore turned her into a meal.
Down the maw of the arachnophobe slid the spider.

Curiosity's cause and effect. A single leg
coughed out by the woken drunk revealing his meal
of the two only me left alive, but somehow the last laugh the spider's.

The Courtship of Noroberto and Guadalupe

It may have been the neon lights reflecting off his pants
but something shone before her eyes, something not quite holy
the night Guadalupe T. Kinsella met Noroberto R. Perchance.

He either said his shoes were damp or else asked her to dance.
Hard for her to tell through the steam of her posole.
(It may just have been neon lights reflecting off his pants.)

A hat of red adorned his head, like a boil to be lanced.
Across his chest he wore a vest the shade of guacamole,
the night Guadalupe T. Kinsella met Noroberto R. Perchance.

His gold tooth grinned as he bowed and showed her most of France,
which chased her stomach to her breast, as if it feared e coli.
Likely, though, it was just the show of neon shine on pants.

He said her eyes of seaweed green had drowned him in a trance.
She was spellbound by his face, his handsome melancholy
the night that Guadalupe T. Kinsella met Noroberto R. Perchance.

In years to come, they would buy a home, have to refinance.
But the future had to wait, for the present moved quite slowly.
Perhaps it was just neon lights reflecting off his pants
but Guadalupe T. would thereafter not be free from
    Señor Noroberto R. Perchance.

When We Lie Down, Again, with Dogs

It could take less than a journey to Wales
more than a trip to your bedroom
to rerail
the train of events
that famously culminated in my shooting your mom.

Nonetheless, I still love you.
And I can't resist posting you this message
from behind the lines of the lost future.

There are barrels of dark purple wine here
and short, silent women who can be bought
for the price of what I used to spend on expensive
coffee.

Still, I would risk capture and extradition
the stupid barking betrayal of my freedom
in order to meet you, casually,
walking up the rainslicked alley on your way home
from the pet supply store.

You have straitjacketed my sense
of what anything is from
and anything else is for.
Please tell your mother I'm sorry.

Yet 2 More Triolets

Cat's Awet
The goddam cat runs down the stairs.
I can't call out his name.
The bastard caught me unawares,
that goddam cat running down the stairs.
He'll sell my stolen tongue to bears
who'll snort it ground with aspartame.
There goes that damn cat down the stairs
and I can't even call his name.

Bad Toupet
Perched on Bill's head like a scared feral cat,
nervous and rangy and losing its fur.
Should've come with a sign: "What are you looking at?"
Perched up on Bill's head like an edgy stray cat.
He drowned it eventually in the muddy South Platte
after some local wise-ass addressed it as "sir."
Perched up there like Uncle Bill's pet feral cat,
nervous and rangy and losing its fur.

Heart of Darkness, Alley behind the 4200 Block of Pearl Street South

His dog the neighbors' Colonel Kurtz
Bloated, insane, and bellowing orders
Corrupted backyards under noon
Sweat runs cold inside our shirts

Bloated maddog bellows orders
Wife in curlers glowers west
Sweat cold running in our shirts
Box of freedom, box of borders

Wife curls her face at the glowering west
Bottle glass browned, sun-shattered glints
Boxes of freedom, boxes of borders
Rust-colored vans come to kill the pest

Bottles browned in sunlight glints
His chores portend his dying first
The vans bring men to kill the pest
In this terminal coincidence

Portents of lawn chores dying first
Corrupted backyards of the noon
This terminal coincidence
His dog the neighbors' Colonel Kurtz

Suppository

Lord when I go
My airy soul
Rising up into the
Thinner and thinner
Layers of atmosphere
Let my smooth and
Yielding flesh
My tubular body
Be pressed
Gently but firmly
Into a small, puckered
Hole in the earth

Rounded end first

Where it can rest
In the warm and fecund
Darkness
And dissolve, slowly
Over time
Yielding vital and healing
Elements to soothe
The angry red bulbs
That arise all too
Often on the troubled surface of the planet.

To a Buick Skylark

Hail dents alight like spit
Birds their nervous worst
From the heavens, or at least their general neighborhood
These profane streams of art

Rust lightening to a golden color
In the false benefit of sunset
And the dissipation of storm clouds
Fleeing from the happy 6 cylinder race

Ground and air for blocks around
Registers the muffler problem
As, when barren evening, clouded by loneliness
Is crowded with your cracked and flowing highbeams

Teach us, car or bird,
What sweet scent shaped of pine
Emanates unhurried
From the place of gloves and wine

(The cans that flood the capture
Are they mine?
Are they mine?)

How indeed can we be glad
This Detroit must know
Not road-weary, traffic mad
No curses from my lips shall flow

And we shall park
In this world
As they are now
Parking before us

Gift of the Ducks, Part 1

I am convinced

like my son is convinced
when jellybeans
appear in the living room

that there will always be
little gifts
left out for us
for little or no reason.

Sometimes right
out in the open
like the two cartons of dog
biscuits left behind
in the warehouse parking lot.

Sometimes hiding
behind a strange sign
like CANNED GOODS CLEARANCE
or SERVICE ROAD.

And, once in a awhile,
given right out in the open,
in front of your entire
political science class,
as with my professor's
announcement that the final exam
was cancelled
due to printing problems
and that we would all get A's
after I had spent
the entire night before
judiciously not studying.

The best so far, though,
has to be
that snowy day,
when you went in to the office to make a few calls.
You were on the phone
with a troubled client
who could not make the drive to see you,
and you glanced over at the window
to see the two ducks
mister and missus
standing on the ledge in the chill,
impatient,
tapping the glass with their noses,

ready to come inside
where they could warm themselves
and tell you
their difficult, but in the end
rather funny tale.

I Become a Victim of Justifiable Catricide

For "Hawkeye"

please excuse me
my disheveled coat and wild-eyed appearance
this morning

but last night
I taunted the sleeping people
within an inch

of my brief hairy life

it was the fat moon
ancient enemy
of cats

dripping its thick
greasy light
through a kitchen window

that stirred my glands again

I howled
like I was born
in the middle country

moved to this place
that smells of wet trees
fruit and salt

the moon is two thousand

miles wide
and the ocean
seven minutes deep

and some nights
I awake with visions
of the edge of the sun

a waterfall of flames larger than a hundred worlds

or all the tuna
fish in the world
behind the bathroom door

just open the door
just open it

Henrys and Elephants

Note: As a boy, my father, Henry Frey, used to lie awake at night listening to the scary animal noises emanating from the Bronx Zoo, several blocks to the east. At the age of three, my son, Henry, fell into the elephant pen at the Denver Zoo, but was fished out by a passing orthodontist.

That which is enormous and enormously distant

I feel like a mouse
lying quietly in my crib
listening to the moonlight bellows
from far away

and consider crying for my mommy

but
something
the end of the cries
which start out so full of size—

a war trumpet to batter the bars that
keep us separated
from those we still love—

who are yet awake and reading
in the next room
or maybe stuck in Gondwanaland
floating southward on the continental drift—

the falling end of those sad notes
humility
we may be enormous
but it is you

you who can fall into our cage
and be lifted out unharmed by a passerby
to wander off where you want to go

to dream and realize giants

Bring Me the Head of Dreadlock Barbie

"O, the truth is, there's a lot being born."—*Traditional folk song*

He is a not yet lost child,
whispers when he talks,
out back on a Friday morning he likes
the quiet before his family awakes.

My early walk around the perimeter
and his own morning ramblings
have led us both out to back corners
of our two adjacent yards.

The intersection between our households
4-foot-tall chain link fence
the deep dog holes, abandoned radial tires
and refuse of a dozen branch-breaking storms.

Weedy and uncared for
like his dirty blond hair
this place is the dark,
wild secret of my suburban backyard.

I am looking for the aged calico
who often stays outside the night through
when I come across the quiet glow
of a different pair of eyes, milk blue.

"Hewwo," his crackly little morning greet.
This child whose name is Matthew,
5-year-old Matthew with the soft sweet
speech impediment—the lisp—

and the sad tolerance for all
the cruelties life will have in store.
Digging in the dawn, damp sandbox and cowboy pajamas
father and mother still inside snoring.

In this clean air,
before the pollution of grownup noise
he is unaware of impossibility.
He is a pilot a bulldozer a cloud a dancing horse.

Crusty nose and snuffles.
"This is Baabie."
Crooked crazy grin and awful
plastic child's trophy

dangling from his dirty fingers
by its stringy Rasta hair.
He is holding a severed head,
shocked doll's face in midair.

"Dweadwock," he croons,
and spins it around him by its locks
in a private-public swoon between two
consenting imaginary animals.

Until a real animal breaks the spell.
Half-blind, black-and-white pit-bull
bounds up, grabs Barbie's head in his powerful jaws,
tears off with it to the other side of the lawn

there to maroon her in the dog shelter
with maybe other members of her species.
So many other discarded toy pieces—
the abandoned, the unfed
denizens of this unmighty backyard society.

Cause Célèbre

In the evening
of the first day
of the second week
of the fifth month
in the fifth year
of the third millennium,

Mumford finally passed his stone.

The stock market
rose almost one hundred points the following day.
A shaky truce in the war
between the world's
religions was reached.
A Korean scientist
accidentally discovered
a vaccine for cellulite.
And the crust of the earth shifted
under Canada
but in a good way
that made the ground feel firmer.

All this happened the following day.

For that one night, though
after he sat
weeping with joy
on the peach ceramic arm of the bathtub,
Mumford,
family and friends
uncorked several bottles
of good champagne,
to toast and rejoice
with such fervor.

As if that one kidney stone
pale and shivering
at the bottom
of the cold toilet bowl
was in fact
the first inhabitant of Earth
to come to land
on the distant dusky surface of Mars.

This Thing about Obituaries

Don't bore the reader
or make me sound better
by bragging about
my postgraduate letters.

And all my good works,
foundations and drives—
leave that for the jerks
who need saints in their lives.

Avoid a description that's
detail sticky:
my Siamese cats,
my granddaughter Vicki . . .

Forget the celebrities
that I knew more or less.
This column's for me.
Let them work for their press.

I want a memorial
that's gritty, mundane.
With whom did I quarrel?
What caused me my pain?

Was I a bastard?
Did I eat paint?
And why did the Coast Guard
have to use those restraints?

If you thought I was gassy,
then list that up front.
If I had a nice chassis—
a fact not to punt.

Did I spit, did I spawn,
leave a stain on the roof?
Did I catch gonorrhea
somewhere north of Duluth?

What kind of glue
did I sniff in the morning?
Did I die quickly or give you
some warning?

Please tell the truth
about that which I loved.
And don't talk about
what I'll do "up above."

And regarding the picture,
you can use what you must.
I'd prefer not the one
from my felony bust.

The Competition

The stars have all been put back up on the shelf
and no one has bothered
to take the sun out of its hatbox yet.

In fact, the brightest light for a hundred yards
is this table lamp
burning from its perch
not on a table but rather an upended
wooden fruit box
which was pressed into service several years ago.

I have been reclining on the purple couch
in this pre-dawn
alternately writing lines of English
in a small blue notebook
and pausing to squint out at
the tableau of a man stretched out
on a couch in the backyard
his notebook disappearing
in the lightening landscape.

The waving forms of nearby pine trees
are the first to emerge
from behind the sofa
as he stops writing and looks up at me.
He turns a bit and I can see
that he's a good looking guy,
wearing a sweatshirt
from my college.
He must have picked it up on sale
however
as the school name has been
mistakenly printed backwards.

A sullen hedge
creeps out of the dark
corner of the yard near his head
where before there had only
been a muted table lamp
and a partially illuminated swath of impossible wall.

Two drunken lawn chairs
are now visible
in a sprawl on the ground
where the wind has left them
but the couch is disappearing
along with my friend in the backyard.
Where does he go in the morning, I wonder.
Does he ever show anybody
that book in which he had been
writing down his thoughts
right-handed, and in Hebrew (I'd have to guess).
Are there any poems in there
about the lazy fellow
who reclines inside the house
each morning
at ease and warm
on the purple sofa?

The Saint of Enclosed Spaces

Such as my skull.

The constant terraforming.

The folds and the flaps of the the brain's surface
a continuous shifting cortical sand dune.

Rivulet gives way to ravine
Joliet becomes Racine
as a memory is startled out of its hiding place.

My father, bless his crinkled soul,
used to call this spelunking: the two of us
talking about a chain of subjects while we
drank our beer from Mexican glass mugs.

His eyes would squish and gleam
when he made the connection between shoes and geometry
the siamese cat and the state of the world.

A turtle crabbing from hillock to hillock
an explorer known to the explored.

This is the place where children play in the dark
but don't bump into the walls.
Not nocturnal—just inside.

Territory of thoughts
memory dream caverns and cauls.

The brown and bended hull of a single popcorn kernel
will contain an entire world
and yet, just as easily plode out—
rupture of life as white and light as a cloud.

Where I Go at Night

In my dreams,
New York is an impossible boulevard
wide as a river.

I am always crossing against traffic
and always across
from an art museum.

San Francisco is a slope.
A vast thicket of train tracks
all of which end
at the bottom of the hill.

Whenever I am there
I ride the smoking engines
horse-straddle
in a rushy panic
as we careen towards the sea.

When I dream of Denver
I am either in
the looming corridors of my grade school
looking for an unlocked door,
or I am flying,
feverish, flapping my arms
to keep from pinwheeling
into the football game
forever taking place behind
my neighbor's red slat fence.

Paris is trickier,
involving not so much
a location as a smell:
rich melted cheese
that drips out of bread
and the feeling of just
having come in from the rain.

When the night takes me
to Santiago de Compostela
it is often in the company of my mother
and either Wayne Newton
or a man claiming to be Wayne Newton.

Mombasa is a room
full of smiling, talking dogs.
And Mumbai, snakes,
ruby striped and not pleased to see me.

In the Hebrides, I repair rock walls.
Low magenta clouds race past.

I never travel to East Asia.
Not Beijing, not Kyoto,
not Changmai, nor Bora-Bora.

But it is that music,
the odd complaining gourd guitar,
the gamelan,
the monstrous drums the size of cars,
that accompanies my dreams of Milwaukee.

Odd that.
I have never actually been to Milwaukee.

When I dream,
as I so often do, of your body,
I am dressed again as a boy scout
about to set off on a hike
through the hilly,
challenging terrain
wearing my old blue
pith helmet
and those silly tan shorts.

Clothesline over Columbus and Kearney

Thirty feet above the rooftop
of the notorious Shadow Club
hangs the underwear
of Mr. Lung, Apt. 3A.

Gray and blue, but mostly white
postcards to the world
his laundry is a heroic gesture
in this just-above space
over the city.

Boxers, briefs,
socks,
how we divided souls
share with each other
our unmentionables.

And just as suddenly
as the city,
two nameless
naked arms grope
out the window to reel
it all back in.

We show up
in your life
and bare all,
yet we will not open
our mouths to say

"Look, I long for your
folding touch.
To stack you on my bed
and bury my face
in your clean rough washcloths.
For the redemption of your warm underpants."

Talking about You #222

For "You-know-who"

Unlike some French director's cue
this should be hard to misconstrue.
Although what's said is nothing new,
I've written a fresh poem for you.

A donkey trip to Katmandu,
a library book long overdue,
a case of Asiatic flu—
none of these compare to you.

To watch a pearl in my shampoo,
or ballet dances by Shamu,
indeed, not even Brunswick stew
uplifts me like the sight of you.

More rapid than bamboo it grew.
Much hotter than a used brake shoe
and higher than Lima, Peru:
this true esteem I feel for you.

My recent upper thigh tattoo
depicting Gerard Depardieu
I've paid the artist to redo
so that the head resembles you.

I'd dunk my head in cheese fondue,
do kung fu with a kangaroo,
cross lava in a bark canoe
if that would bring a smile to you.

I'd spend a year writing haiku,
climb K2 in my pink muumuu,
perfect my chicken cordon bleu
to demonstrate my hots for you.

An analytical review
of what my love has put me through
might help you find you like me too
and stop saying that I'm stalking you.

You'll be glad to know the A.C.L.U
has lined my case up in their queue.
Though it's a shame—this need to sue—
I'll do it for a date with you.

Walks into a Bar

"Stop me if you've heard this one."

A man walks into a bar.
Bartender says, "What'll y'have?"
Man says "A martini, please."
Tender replies, "Good, because that's all we serve."

A dog walks into a bar.
Barks out an order for a martini.
Bartender tells him he doesn't serve
wiener-dogs.
Dog corrects him, pointing out
that he is correctly called a "Dachshund."
The martini is served.

A rabbit walks into a bar.
Orders a mai-tai.
Bartender corrects him.
This joke only serves martinis.

Two priests walk into a bar.
Order two martinis
and leave without paying.

Two dentists walk into a bar.
As they lift their martinis,
one says to the other,
"Open wide!"

Two lovers walk into a bar
there to encounter
not only the bartender,
who is a former lover of the first lover,
but also martinis,
the first love of the second lover.

A kangaroo and an insurance salesman
hop and walk
simultaneously yet separately
into a bar.
They do not speak to each other
while drinking their martinis.
Later the kangaroo is overheard
arguing about the bill with the bartender.

A single, 40-year-old man
and his mother
walk into a bar
where they run into a young single woman
who coincidentally works in the same office
as the mother
and who was only yesterday
engaged in an animated lunchtime conversation
with the mother about her single, 40-year-old son.
The two women chat happily over martinis.
The man glumly watches college basketball
and wishes this was the kind of bar that sold beer
instead of just martinis.

Jesus and his mother
walk into a bar.
The bartender comps their drinks.

Henry Ford, Orville Wright, and Neil Armstrong
walk into a bar.
Over martinis they discuss
the one subject about which all three can agree:
the 1980 Winter Olympics in Lake Placid, NY.

Mr. Ed, the talking horse, and his entourage
walk into a bar.
The entourage drinks martinis.
Mr. Ed eats their olives.

Zarathustra, Nebuchadnezzar, and Gilgamesh
walk into a bar.
They are soon joined by many other
glorious priests and kings of old.
Nobody's credit card goes through,
so Gilgamesh has to pay for everyone's
martinis with the Royal Golden Sceptre of Uruk.

Three poets walk into a bar.
They order martinis
and sit around dissecting jokes
just to watch them twitch on the tabletop.

Post-modern Irony walks into a bar,
asks the bartender whether
Neo-Classicism has been in today.
Leaves without ordering a drink.
The bartender does not show up for work the next day.

Wilbik

I am a wilbik tree.
I am a wilbik tree's enemy.
I am a wilbik tree.
I am a wilbik tree's enemy.

I am the squirrel in the wilbik tree.
I am the enemy of that squirrel.
I am the squirrel in the wilbik tree.
I am the enemy of that squirrel.

I am a wilbik nut that feeds the squirrel.
I am a wilbik nut's worst enemy.
I am a wilbik nut that feeds the squirrel.
I am a wilbik nut's worst enemy.

I am bad taste.
I am obsessive repetition.
I am nut paste,
damned to perdition.